SHIMMERING STONES

SHIMMERING STONES

An interactive guide to Queensland's Gemfields

CLARE MILES ANDERSEN

Clare Miles Andersen

ACKNOWLEDGEMENTS

Gratitude fills every fiber of my being as I acknowledge those whose unwavering support has been my steadfast anchor throughout this journey. Firstly, to my patient and supportive husband Josh, whose enduring encouragement ignites the flames of my passion projects. To my son Miles, your candid honesty mirrors that of your mother and for that I am deeply thankful.

My heartfelt appreciation extends to my astute sister Ruth, whose keen eye for detail ensures no punctuation or grammar error escapes her scrutiny. To my beautiful niece Ava, your graciousness in allowing me to use your likeness on the cover is a gift beyond measure.

In addition, I am indebted to my best friend Kellie-Jo whose friendship and sage advice have been invaluable, transcending distance and time. To my beloved parents Phil and Di, your nurturing guidance has shaped me in profound ways, anchoring me in the unique beauty of this corner of the world. Despite my youthful eagerness to explore beyond its borders, adulthood has illuminated the tranquil splendor and richness of life amidst the bush.

Returning home to the Gemfields annually is a pilgrimage of the heart, where I am greeted with open arms by old friends and welcomed into the embrace of new connections. In the warmth of its people and amidst the brilliance of its sparkling gems I find myself forever captivated, forever grateful.

CONTENTS

Acknowledgements v
WELCOME ix

   1 LANDSCAPES   1
   2 SAPPHIRES   4
   3 MINING   8
   4 DWELLINGS   12
   5 DUNNIES   15
   6 ANIMALS   19
   7 ADVENTURES   23
   8 EVENTS   27
   9 SIGNS   33
  10 SIGHTS   36

Chapter 6 Animal Activity Correct Answers 41
Author Bio 43
Photos Of Clare's Early Years 44

WELCOME

You will need a pencil or pen and some coloured pencils to complete the activities.
You may also like to print photographs and glue them in.

This book belongs to (your name)

....

I am ....years old.

The day/month and year is...

I am visiting/living at the Gemfields with

....

....

The best thing about being here is

....

....

....

....

....

CHAPTER 1

LANDSCAPES

One day, we embarked on a grand and thrilling plan
to explore Australia's beauty, an adventurous span
through sights and glory, we'd roam and roam
until we reached the Gemfields, our new-found home

in our car, caravan in tow we journeyed wide
our house on wheels, where memories reside
beds, chairs, a sink and a fridge to hold delights
bouncing on the dusty road, with jerks and flights

through clouds of dust, we ventured near and far
the old road led us beneath the twinkling star
corrugations and twists, the path was rough
but determination held us, we were made of tough

caught in 'Gem fever,' the allure had its hold
stories of treasures and tales, some remain untold
a dirt plot we chose, where a family base would rise
mining for sapphires, our pursuit would energise

bushes, trees and rustling bugs, a symphony of sound
shadows danced and silence echoed all around
brushing away flies with the great 'Aussie wave'
in this rugged land, adventures cherished and saved

with my faithful companion Zed, by my side
a German Shepherd, his loyalty my guide
excitement overwhelmed; I leapt out to explore
greeted by stillness, dirt and bush galore

we were undeterred, for this was our chance
to create a life of adventure in this great expanse
at the Gemfields, our dreams would be fulfilled
among dirt and scrub, our destiny instilled.

On the next page inside the frame draw a scene of the bush at the Gemfields.

You may like to include any animals you have seen.

CHAPTER 2

SAPPHIRES

In the Gemfields, a vast and wondrous place
Anakie, Sapphire, Rubyvale and The Willows interlace
from distant lands people journey far and wide
to witness nature's gems, to find riches outside

some come to stay just for a little while
to dig and explore with a hopeful smile
others seek fortune, to strike it rich
dreaming of treasures not yet found, an alluring pitch

once unearthed, these precious stones of colours rare
are sorted with precision, with upmost care
blues, yellows, oranges, pinks and greens all gleaming bright
and parti colours, a blend of shades, a mesmerising sight

but sapphires are not alone, other treasures await
zircons, spinal, gold nuggets or diamonds are also great
cut or polished in settings they'll gleam
transformed into beauty, like a radiant dream

not every gem can be cut due to imperfections and size
even a polished stone can be a nice surprise
shapes are diverse like the stars above
round, pear, emerald and heart, the symbol of love

rose, trillion, brilliant, marquise and oval
each unique and captivating, sure to make you jovial
The Gemfields, a realm of dreams where riches lie
a place where magic dwells beneath the vast sky

people come from afar; the earth's secrets to untwine
in this enchanting land, where precious treasures shine
I hope you find your own sapphire to keep
look at the surface, some are not that deep.

Colour all the different cut shapes of sapphires in your favourite colours.

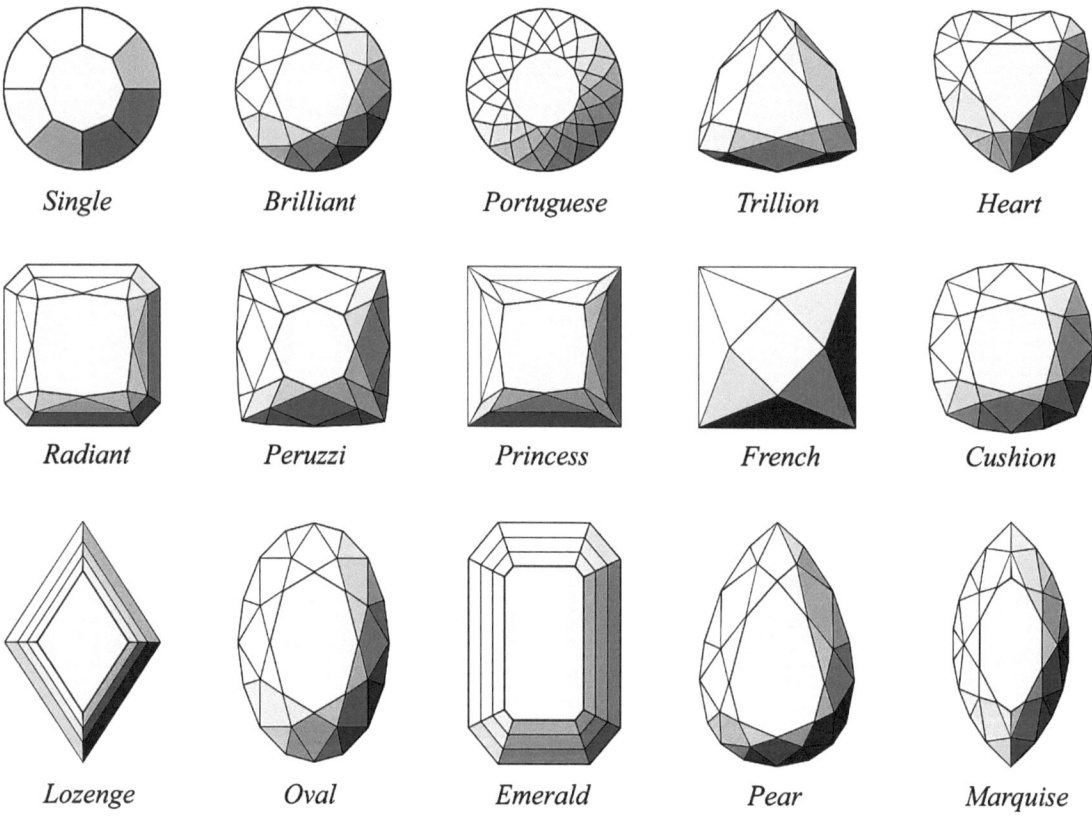

SHIMMERING STONES - 7

See if you can work out the colour of each gem and put into the crossword. The answers are at the bottom upside down.

1.YELLOW, 2.RED, 3.WHITE, 4.TURQUOISE, 5.LIME, 6.CRIMSON, 7.AQUA, 8.GREEN, 9.BLUE, 10.LAVENDER, 11.PINK

CHAPTER 3

MINING

Mining sapphires, tools in hand you stand
or machines in a setup that's grand
both demand hard work and patience too
with energy spent and plenty of sweat all day through

sometimes tears of joy, others of despair
a mix of emotions you must be aware
blood may be drawn, luck is your guide
in this gem-hunting journey chance will decide

above ground the sun rays scorch the land
below coolness prevails to avoid becoming over tanned
no room for claustrophobia, strength is the key
safety first, to mine responsibly brings glee

amidst the clamour of shovels, picks and more
jackhammers echo, a resonant roar
pulsators pulse and buckets fill fast
an orchestra of mining, a specialist craft

embrace the dust, the dirt and the mud
find a big sapphire, your face will be smug
with water's help the wash is set right
the lighter rocks flow, the gems gleam in sight

yet despite all efforts, a moment of strain
agitation may creep like passing rain
but the sapphires await in the wash, ready to gleam
in this gem-filled world, a miner's dream.

Here are some photos of how my family mined for sapphires on the Gemfields.

On the next page help the boy collect as many gems as possible on his way to the giant one at the end of the maze.

SHIMMERING STONES — 11

CHAPTER 4

DWELLINGS

Indeed the buildings here are a sight to behold
what unique and creative stories they've told
dwellings, camps, caravans, houses and sheds
a tapestry of architecture, where life threads

beside the mine shaft, covered in iron's embrace
some barely a shelter, a humpy in the scrub's grace
surrounded by grass, shrubs and trees
at harmony with nature, far from the sea

creative designs like artwork they stand
occupied in winter in this captivating land
my parents' house is made from billy boulder rocks
hard, compact, water-worn and hard to chop

stacked with concrete they stand strong like new
in fires they won't explode, just split, it's true
various sizes and shapes, like sapphires gleam
building dreams, fulfilling each gem-filled theme

ironbark timber, galvanized iron with might
rocks, clay and wire, each construction's a delight
coloured glass bottles, a splash of hue
materials recycled and given life anew.

Inside the frame on the next page draw your favourite humpy you have seen while exploring the Gemfields.

CHAPTER 5

DUNNIES

Have you seen those loos, so wild and bold?
a rainbow of colours, stories untold
purples, greens, pinks and blues
in this quirky world they sure do amuse

corrugated iron with bottles and shells they blend
plastic, wood and bells are the trend
shapes and sizes, oh how they vary
imagination runs wild, not one that's ordinary

materials abundant, at hand they're found
cracked, sun weathered, rising from the ground
each one with a story to tell
in this quirky realm, where wonders dwell.

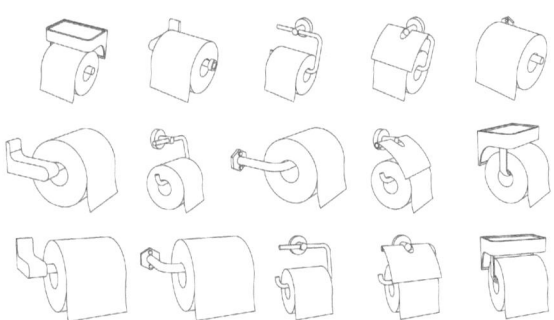

Here are some photos of the various dunnies found in the bush at the Gemfields.

SHIMMERING STONES - 17

Colour in and add decorations to this outback loo.

CHAPTER 6

ANIMALS

From microscopic geckos to creatures of size
tall emus and cows, a grand sight for the eyes
some with friendliness, from your hand they'll feed
like brushtail possums and lorikeets in need

a variety of birds, colours in the air
in formations they soar, blocking sunlight with flair
white cockatoos screech with voices so bold
among long grass, kangaroos leap and unfold

blending with the surroundings, hidden by their guise
over fences they bound under open skies
mums and bubs pop out, a quick shy "Hi!"
camels, wild horses and goats passing by

tallest among creatures, the camels stand
with towering grace, smiles vast and grand
they grumble and spit, a curious sight
drawing flies by thousands, day and night

insects aplenty, annoying they swarm
from ants to mossies, causing a storm
of discomfort and itch, a bothersome spree
both nibble your skin, humming with glee

out in this land pets find their place
dogs wag their tails, feline friends grace
chickens and roosters a common view
exotic pets too, some choose to pursue

peacocks in glory, guinea fowl unique
unusual companions, the bold and mystique
yet snakes, oh no, they're not my desire
I'd much prefer the creatures less dire

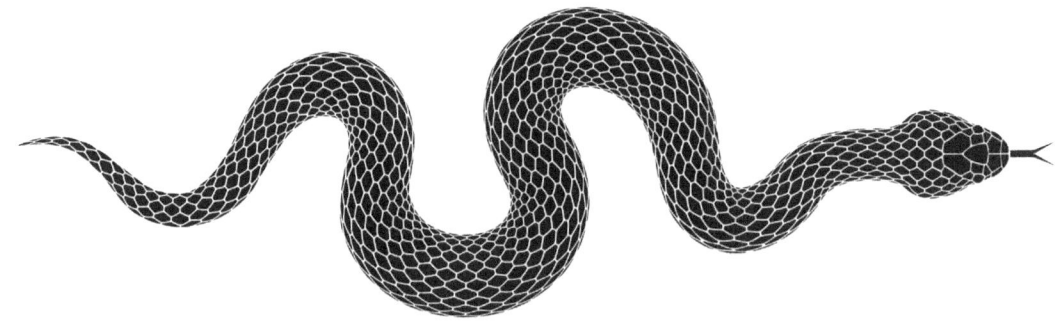

wallabies' petite, smaller than kangaroos in size
they hop and they swim, crawl under skies
a pace they pick up, feet flying over the ground
in the wild, dingoes roam untamed and all around

on crown land animals roam devouring all green
at night echidnas surface, a curious scene
up from the ground, borrowing through
devouring flowers, my mum's work they undo

owls hoot and survey, their watchful eyes wide
seeking insects and crickets with sounds as their guide
in this chorus of life strange creatures make you smile
countless wonders to see, both gentle and wild.

Whose poo is whose? Draw a line to match up the animal and its poo.
Correct answers are in the back of the book.

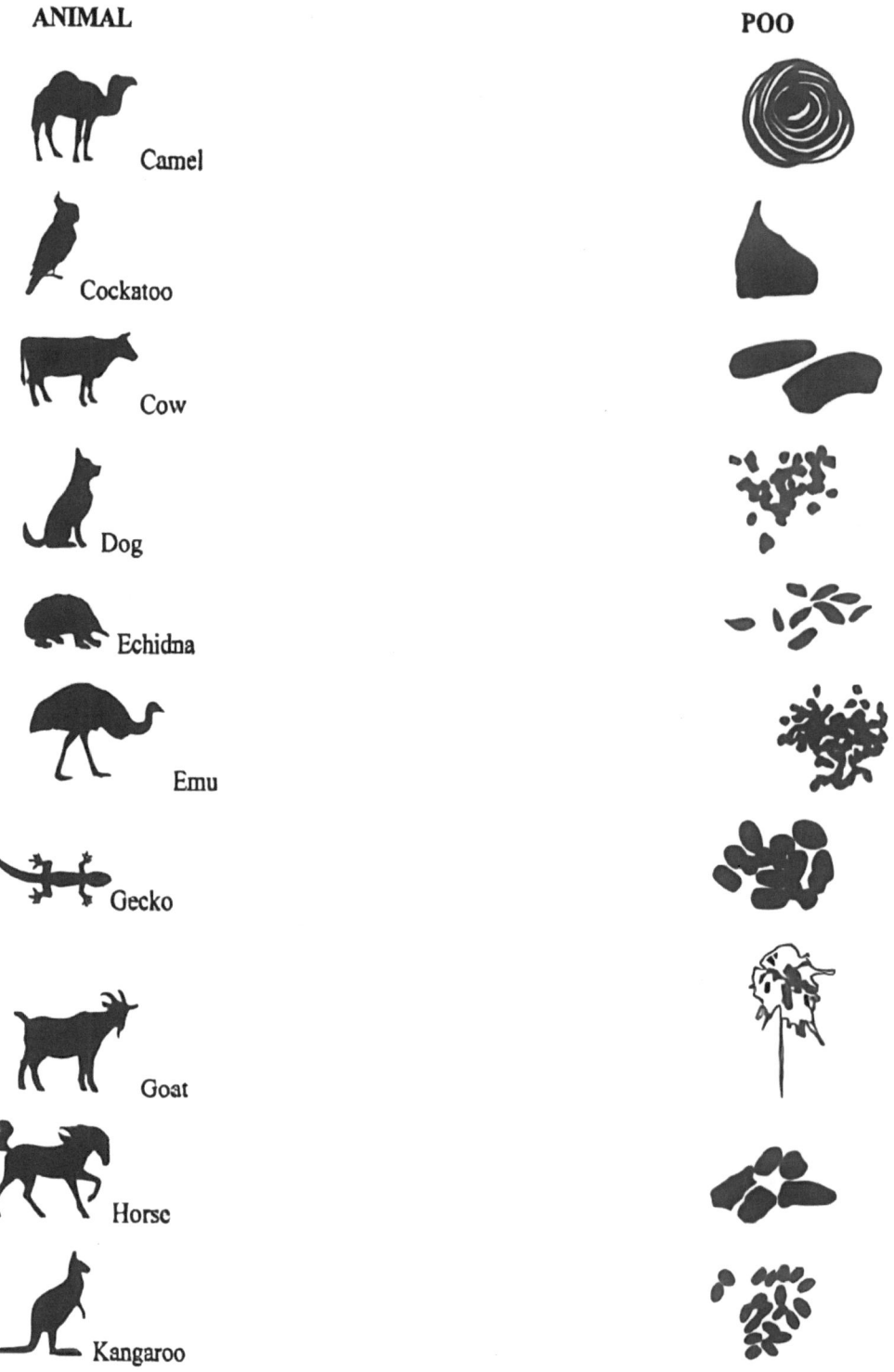

CHAPTER 7

ADVENTURES

You might glance around finding not much to do
except seek sapphires and dabble in dry creek beds too
but depending on your age and the time of year
there are many interesting things to do if the sky is clear

growing up in this place my pals and I'd pedal all day
unveiling dirt paths, relishing sights along the way
after breakfast we'd vanish, return with twilight's grace
we'd plunge in dams to cool off, loving the embrace

kids tethering ropes to trees like monkeys, they'd sway
mud flinging and clowning, laughing whilst we play
car tyres swung high, makeshift swings in the breeze
down flooded creeks we'd voyage, wherever they'd seize

when a youngster, I'd while away hours toy cars in hand
sis and I, creek games, imagination our band
'treasures' we'd gather from leaves, feathers and bone
pet rocks aplenty, each one a keepsake, our own

in a wheelbarrow, we'd jostle and jest
now Rubyvale shelters a playground, the best
sapphire boasts a pool and skate park delight
grown older, bold ventures, motorbike flight

on horseback, the thrill of the journey ahead
cubby houses and tree forts out spread
fun takes its form in this bushland retreat
sitting, absorbing, nature's rhythm discreet

mine tours subterranean, markets that gleam
sport clubs that rally making a team
dining spots special where flavors unite
billboards along trails, facts sparking insight

fossicking still charms where washes and tides interlock
to easily find your fortune visit a sapphire-filled shop
or trek a trail in pursuit of the gem that is rare
tourist trinkets galore are found in corner stores ware

Policeman's Knob, a hike often embraced
the timeless view never leaves us disgraced
come night, the Milky Way and planets so bright
observatories beckon, a celestial delight.

On the next page colour in the tree house in whatever colours you like.

CHAPTER 8

EVENTS

Each year people travel far and wide
to come and celebrate sapphires with pride
there are markets and stalls aplenty, side by side
horse buggy rides, bouncy castles for the kids, don't hide

once upon a time there was a famous wheelbarrow race
you had no choice but to keep up the pace
running 16.2km with a barrow, billy, shovel and pick
halfway swapped the billy to a bag of wash, a real kick!

mostly men bumping each other's shoulders in a race
training for months, goal of finishing, a real chase
you needed lots of stamina and grit
sweat, tears, torn muscles, heat stroke, the body took a hit

not for just anyone is running on bitumen and dirt
you could end up with sore knees and really get hurt
lots of huffing and puffing with little grace
some people gave up and just stopped in their place

the race was won more than once by the same familiar face
great to see so many people joining in haste
fun continued with chainsaw comps and wood chopping
the noisy bulldozer fight would have all the kids hopping

a boat regatta in the dry creek bed, a hard race
boats made of anything found lying around the place
bottles, cans, cardboard surrounds and old sheets for sails
hand painted, funny names, make us laugh and wail

for the young and the old a traditional sack race game
and catch the greasy pig if you dare was the main aim
some would get on the slippery log
to push each other off into a muddy bog

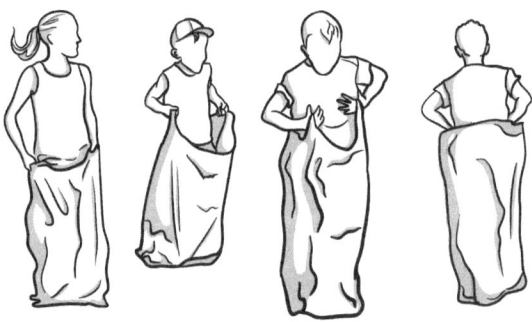

the Gem Festival had fancy dress for adults and kids alike
my parents created and painted their costumes at night
there would be a theme everyone would have to adhere
a parade for you to be judged the best by your peers

at night the sky would fill with crackling fire
an enormous bonfire with fallen tree trunks, built prior
juicy sizzling meat on a spit if you should desire
food, the usual festival fare, much to admire

people organised on chairs to improve their viewing luck
music bands bleating out tunes from a flatbed truck
fireworks the highlight of the night, the sky on fire
adults sing along, dogs howling too, some never tired

the best part for some would be the Billy Cart race
down Shell Hill in Rubyvale, best to protect your face
carts homemade contraptions, some thrilling
household chairs, bathtubs and beds for the willing

every colour and material you could imagine in fashion
put together with wire, tape and passion
turned into rockets with wheels and little brakes
lots of cheering and laughter, sometimes mistakes

steering using rope and ladders to avoid smashes
often bumps, spills and more than a few crashes
grazes, skin missing, blood spilled, carts destroyed
bruises to show off during school time, kids overjoyed!

Look at the pictures of all the different types of Billy Carts.
Inside the frame on the next page, design and colour in your own.

CHAPTER 9

SIGNS

One thing I love so much around the Gemfields land
different signs and statues you can find if you have a plan
some in plain sight and others hidden away
off the beaten track if you want to seek them and play

the hills have many shop signs, most no longer around
promises in faded colours of gems abound
your head will fly in all directions, you'll feel hit with a hammer
in Sapphire a sign asking, 'nuts tightened at the big spanner?'

shops display the wonders of jewellery and sapphire
if you make time to stop, you too will feel the fire
from the famous gem shop under the giant ring
get a cool photo, perhaps showing off some new bling!

and let's not forget the sign that states where you are
the 'Tropic of Capricorn' is right here, you are far
it marks the most southern latitude for the sun
directly overhead at noon, knowledge is such fun

everywhere signs scream 'back off', 'stay away', 'beware'!
and other not so polite ways to give you a scare
telling you a mining claim is below and not to bother
don't step, don't look, do not hover!

"Stub your toe on a fortune", as you say goodbye
hopefully be back to embrace this wonder, time can fly
come bring your friends and children to discover
this interesting place with gems still left to uncover

experience the Sapphire Gemfields Treasure Trail
a self-guided tour, the history of this place, listen to a tale
interpretive signage and solar-powered audio posts
I wonder which one you will enjoy the most?

Inside the frame on the next page draw and colour in all the different signs you have seen.

SHIMMERING STONES — 35

CHAPTER 10

SIGHTS

In Rubyvale meet 'Bobby Dazzler', a man of pleasure
a sapphire shop, mine tour or fossick to find a treasure
expand your travels along a rough dirt road
find the 'thong tree', a hint below to help your mental load

near Policeman's Knob an old volcano you should find
I climb it every time, it's a great way to unwind
be sure to get a photo to prove you climbed up
and show it to your friends, apparently it's good luck

the 'New Rubyvale Hotel' pub is an iconic destination
burnt down, moved, re-built, there is an explanation
a movie made here, 'Buddies' you should try to watch
it is great family fun; I find it top notch

you should be able to easily spot
the minion as he sits atop
an old car, deliberately buried partly in the ground
'Buckingham Palace' next door is found

the 'Miners Heritage' is another great place to discover
where you can walk underground, be cool undercover
they explain finding sapphires by hand or machine
fossick for your own gems, fun even if you are a teen

with wash, you will be helped and inspired
find a precious sapphire to keep and admire
a few observatories you may be able to uncover
one called the 'Gemeye', it's my dad's you may discover

if you stay awake after dark and look up you might see
the delights of the Southern Cross, but no guarantee
out here you will find many heavenly sights
a magically filled starry night sky shedding light

there is petrol, food and drinks at the local stores
inside contains fossicking gear and affordable gifts galore
staff are super friendly and will make time for you
to ask any question or get directions they will be true

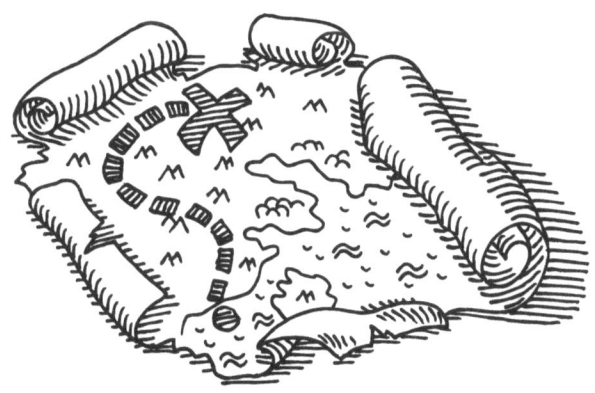

the 'Salvation Army' a billy boulder shop, have a look
trinkets and treasures, from board games to books
if you find yourself bothered by the rain or sun
plenty of clothing for summer and winter, looking is fun

there is even a hardware store with all sorts of things
make your visit more comfortable and feel like a king
a post office in each town to send cards to friends
and a noticeboard outside, not just selling gems

be sure to visit the Wetland Reserve, a 14 hectare area
in the wet season you will see it is the more the merrier
so many different bird appearances and sounds
giant Brolgas to tiny ones hidden on the ground

in Anakie you will see something beautiful and bright
a colourful glass sculpture, spectacular in the sunlight
'Sapphire Reflections', an artistic tribute to here
it stands proud at the crossroads for all to see and cheer

the very old cemetery has fancy iron lace adding glee
and the Anakie Railway station has a famous bottle tree
helping us to remember an important time in history
if you visit and read, you will discover the mystery

the best thing by far is meeting the locals
big personalities with very loud vocals
the people and animals make the Gemfields so neat
it is a unique location, one to embrace with dirty feet

most likely this place is one you won't soon forget
filled with laughter and a treasure or two you have kept
I hope it won't be the last time you will explore
be sure to tell your friends all about it please, I implore

you may even like to recommend this book
to share, to learn, to get Gemfields hooked
be sure to finish all the pages within
one day you will look back and I bet you grin!

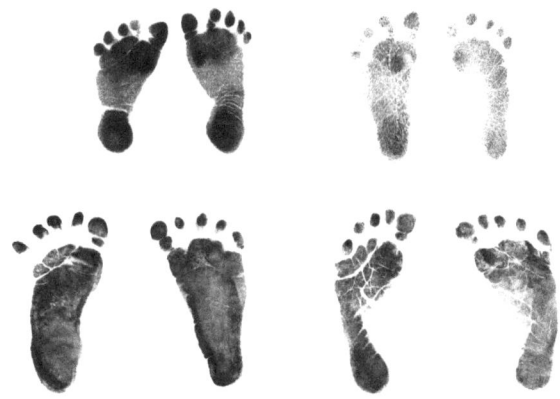

Write about your most memorable Gemfields adventure.

CHAPTER 6 ANIMAL ACTIVITY CORRECT ANSWERS

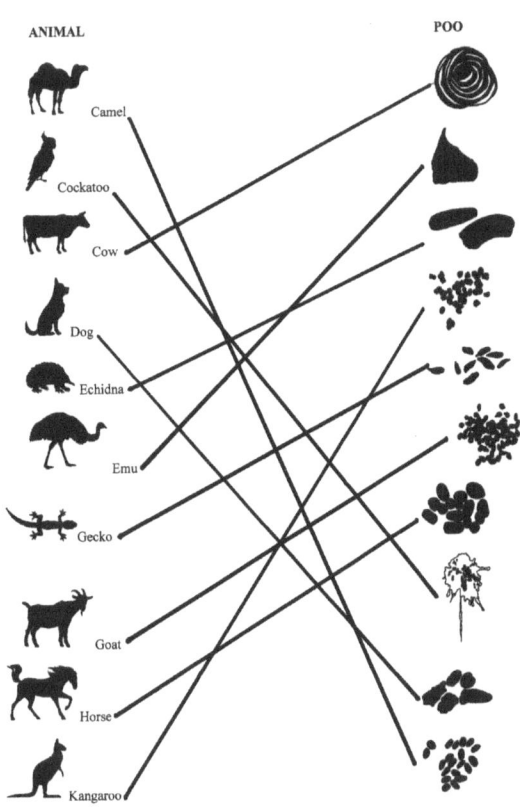

AUTHOR BIO

Clare's journey began in 1975, as she arrived in Rubyvale with her family from Adelaide when she was just a baby. Growing up amidst the rugged beauty of the Gemfields, her childhood was marked by the hum of her father's sapphire mining endeavours, spent in the cozy confines of a caravan. In 1979, her family welcomed her sister Ruth into their midst, further enriching their tight-knit bond.

Over the years, amidst the dust and gemstones, Clare's parents laid down roots, slowly crafting a remarkable three-bedroom billy boulder house atop Bedford Hill, a testament to their perseverance and dedication. This cherished home still stands proudly today, a symbol of their enduring connection to the land.

Educated in the heart of the Gemfields, Clare and her sister attended Anakie Primary School before continuing their academic journey at Emerald High School. However, the call of broader horizons beckoned, and at 17 they bid farewell to their gem-laden surroundings to pursue higher education at university.

For Clare, this journey led her to delve into her passions for photography and education, eventually blossoming into a career as a high school teacher. Yet, no matter where life took her, the allure of Rubyvale remained strong, pulling her back time and again.

Today, while Clare's parents still call Rubyvale home, she and her sister Ruth, along with their husbands and children, return every winter eager to share their love of adventure and the enchanting wonders of the Gemfields. Through their annual visits, they continue to weave new memories in this gem-studded landscape and deepen their connection to this vibrant community, ensuring that the legacy of their upbringing endures for generations to come.

PHOTOS OF CLARE'S EARLY YEARS

Behold these captivating glimpses of Clare's early years blossoming amidst the enchanting landscapes of the Gemfields.